STORMS

WEATHER REPORT

Ann and Jim Merk

The Rourke Corporation, Inc.
Vero Beach, Florida 32964

PHOTO CREDITS
© Wyman Meinzer: pages 10, 15, 21; © Lynn M. Stone: title page,
pages 7, 8, 12, 18; courtesy South Dakota Tourism: cover;
courtesy National Oceanic and Atmospheric Administration: pages
4, 17; courtesy NASA: page 13

Library of Congress Cataloging-in-Publication Data

Merk, Ann, 1952–
    Storms / by Ann and Jim Merk.
        p. cm. — (Weather report)
    Includes index
    ISBN 0-86593-386-3
    1. Storms—Juvenile literature. 2. Weather—Juvenile literature.
[1. Storms.]
I. Merk, Jim, 1952- . II. Title   III. Series: Merk, Ann, 1952- Weather
report.
QC941.3.M47 1994
551.55—dc20   94-13321
                                                            CIP
Printed in the USA   AC

TABLE OF CONTENTS

STORMS

Weather is always changing. Some days are warm and sunny. Other days may be cloudy and cool.

Sometimes the weather is unsettled and "ornery," or stormy. Stormy weather brings **precipitation**, and it may bring strong winds.

Storms can be frightening. They may cause tremendous damage to buildings, highways, vehicles, power stations and crops. Storms can also injure and kill people.

Storms like this tornado can be dangerous and deadly

RAINSTORMS

In some parts of the United States they are called "gulley washers." Elsewhere they are just rainstorms. Whatever they're called, rainstorms can be dangerous when they cause flooding.

Flooding occurs when the ground and streams can no longer hold rain. If too much rain falls too fast, the ground cannot soak it up. Larger and larger pools form. Rivers and streams overflow their banks and pour into the surrounding ground.

6

Hard rainstorms, like this one over the Badlands of South Dakota, can cause sudden "flash" floods

THUNDERSTORMS

Thunderstorms are loud, windy storms with lightning and rain. Sometimes they make **hail**.

A thunderstorm is born when the sun heats the ground and forces warm, wet air to rise. When the warm air meets colder, drier air, thunderclouds form.

Thunderclouds can produce heavy rain. Sometimes the raindrops within the clouds are blown upward into cooler air. Then they form balls of ice—hail.

Thunderstorms produce heavy rain, lightning, thunder and sometimes hail

ELECTRIC STORMS

Every thunderstorm carries electricity, or lightning, with it. But some thunderstorms pack an unusually great amount of lightning.

Lightning bolts can travel between clouds, inside clouds or between a cloud and the ground. Lightning that strikes the ground is extremely dangerous.

The heat produced by lightning causes the air around it to become extremely hot. This super-heated air explodes outward, making the booms called thunder. Thunder is loud, but not dangerous.

Lightning bolts can be extremely dangerous as they reach to the ground

Freezing rain turns lawns and roadways into a slick sheet of glassy ice

A satellite view of a hurricane showing its "eye" in the center

TORNADOES

A tornado is a powerful, swirling windstorm. It forms a black, funnel-shaped cloud. Tornadoes can develop when the winds moving upward in a large thunderstorm begin to swirl.

As it rushes through the air, a tornado spins like a child's top. The twisting "tail" of the tornado may dip to earth. When it does, it may destroy almost everything it touches in its narrow path.

A twisting tornado dances toward the ground

HURRICANES

A hurricane is a large wind and rainstorm that forms over oceans. The hurricane grows in a doughnut shape that can be several hundred miles wide. The doughnut hole is the hurricane's "eye."

A hurricane has powerful winds of at least 75 miles per hour. By the time a hurricane reaches land, it can have winds well over 100 miles per hour.

Land takes the punch away from a hurricane. As hurricanes move inland, they weaken quickly.

*Hurricane winds lash a
southern seashore*

BLIZZARDS

A blizzard is a snowstorm driven by strong winds. Along with blowing snow, blizzards may bring frigid temperatures.

People have a difficult time driving or walking in a blizzard. Blowing snow can hide almost everything from view. That creates a condition known as a **whiteout**.

A true blizzard has winds of more than 32 miles per hour.

Protected by heavy fur, a wolf does little more than blink at the fury of a winter storm

STORMS WITH ICE

Summer hailstorms can punish the ground with icy "stones" the size of peas, golfballs or even baseballs! Hail is a combination of ice and snow.

Sleet, which falls during cold weather, is a form of ice.

Sometimes during winter the ground is much colder than the air. Rain can turn to ice upon contact with the ground. This "freezing rain" covers everything it touches with a **glaze** of ice.

Falling hailstones can easily damage cars and buildings

FORECASTING STORMS

Weather can change quickly. That makes it difficult to **forecast**, or predict, a storm and its path.

It is important, though, that scientists *try* to predict storms. Knowing where and when storms may strike can save property and lives.

In the United States the National Weather Service regularly broadcasts news about dangerous weather. Satellites, **radar** and computers help weather scientists predict storms.

Glossary

forecast (FOR kast) — to predict, especially to predict the weather

glaze (GLAYZ) — a smooth, glassy surface of ice caused by rain freezing upon contact with cold ground or objects

hail (HAIL) — the balls of snow and ice, in varying sizes, that may be produced by a thunderstorm

precipitation (pre sip uh TAY shun) — rain, snow and sleet

radar (RAY dar) — system in which sound wave echoes are used to locate distant objects in the air

whiteout (WHITE out) — blinding conditions created by blowing or falling snow

INDEX